I0427124

Mastering Bolshevism
Joseph Stalin

This edition first printed June 2021.

ISBN: 978-1-304-07375-4

Mastering Bolshevism

Joseph Stalin

TABLE OF CONTENTS

Forward

Comrades!

From the reports and the debates on these reports heard at this plenum*, it is evident that we are dealing with the following three main facts.

First, the wrecking and diversionist-espionage work of agents of foreign countries, among whom a rather active role was played by the Trotskyists, affected more or less all, or nearly all, of our organizations-economic, administrative, and Party.

Second, agents of foreign countries, among them the Trotskyites, penetrated not only into lower organizations, but also into certain responsible posts.

Third, some of our leading comrades, both at the center and at the periphery, not only failed to discern the face of these wreckers, diversionists, spies, and killers, but proved to be so careless, complacent,and naive that at times they themselves assisted in promoting agents of foreign states to responsible posts.

These are the three incontrovertible facts which naturally emerge from the reports and the discussions on them.

• Report to the Plenum of the Central Committee of the RKP(b), March 3, 1937.

I. POLITICAL CARELESSNESS

How are we to explain the fact that our leading comrades, having a rich experience in the struggle against all sorts of anti-Party and anti-Soviet currents, proved in the present case to be so naive and blind that they were unable to discern the real face of the enemies of the people, that they failed to recognize the wolves in sheep's clothing and were unable to tear away their masks?

Can it be claimed that the wrecking and diversionist-espionage work of the agents of foreign states operating in the territory of the USSR can be anything unexpected and unprecedented for us? No, it is impossible to claim this. This is demonstrated by the wrecking acts in various branches of the national economy during the past ten years, beginning in the Shakhty period, as recorded in official documents.

Can it be claimed that in this past period there were no precautionary signals or warnings about the wrecking, spying, or terrorist activities of the Trotskyist-Zinovievist agents of fascism? No, it is impossible to claim this. We had such signals, and Bolsheviks have no right to forget about them.

The foul murder of Comrade Kirov was the first serious warning which indicated that enemies of the people would resort to double-dealing and that they would mask themselves as Bolsheviks, as Party members, in order to worm their way into our confidence and to thus open access for themselves into our organizations.

The trial of the "Leningrad Center," as well as the "Zinoviev-Kamenev" trial, gave new grounds for the lessons following from the foul murder of Comrade Kirov.

The trial of the "Zinovievist-Trotskyist Bloc" broadened the lessons of the preceding trials and demonstrated before our eyes that the Zinovievites and Trotskyites had united around themselves every hostile bourgeois element; that they had turned into an espionage, diversionist-terrorist agency of the German secret police; that double-dealing and masking themselves are the only means by which the Zinovievites and Trotskyites can penetrate into our organizations; that vigilance and political insight are the surest means of preventing such penetration and for liquidation of the Zinovievist-Trotskyist gang.

The Central Committee of the RKP(b) in its January 18, 1935 confidential letter on the foul killing of Comrade Kirov, emphatically warned Party organizations against political complacency and narrow-minded empty-headedness. That confidential letter stated:

"We must put a stop to the opportunistic complacency which arises from the mistaken assumption that as we grow in the strength of our forces, our enemies become ever more tame and harmless. Such an assumption is fundamentally wrong. It is an echo of the the Right deviation, which assured all and sundry that the enemies would quietly creep into Socialism, that they would become real Socialists in the end. Bolsheviks must not rest on their laurels and become empty-headed. We

12

do not need complacency, but vigilance, real Bolshevik, revolutionary vigilance. We must remember that the more hopeless the position of the enemies becomes, the more readily they will clutch at extreme measures as the only measures of the doomed in their struggle against Soviet power. One must remember this and be vigilant."

In its confidential letter of July 29, 1936, on the espionage-terrorist activities of the Trotskyist-Zinovievist bloc, the Central Committee of the RKP(b) once again called upon Party organizations to display the utmost vigilance, the ability to discern enemies of the people, no matter how well masked they may be. The confidential letter stated:

"Now that it has been proved that the Trotskyist-Zinovievist fiends are uniting in the struggle against Soviet power all the most infuriated and vicious enemies of the toilers of our country-the spies, provocateurs, diversionists, whiteguards, kulaks, and so on; when all boundaries have been obliterated between these elements on the one hand and the Trotskyists and Zinovievists on the other; all of our Party organizations and all members of the Party must understand that vigilance on the part of Communists is imperative on every sector and under all circumstances. The inalienable quality of every Bolshevik under present conditions must be the ability to discern an enemy of the Party, no matter how well masked he may be."

And so there were signals and warnings.

What did these signals and warnings call for?

They called for the elimination of the weakness of Party organizational work and for the transformation of the Party into an impregnable fortress into which not a single double-dealer could penetrate.

They called upon us to put a stop to the underestimation of Party-political work and to make an emphatic turn towards the utmost strengthening of such work, towards the strengthening of political vigilance.

And what happened? The facts show that the signals and warnings were heeded very slowly by our comrades.

This was eloquently demonstrated by the well-known facts revealed in the course of the campaign for the verification and exchange of Party documents.

How are we to explain the fact that these warnings and signals did not have their proper effect?

How are we to explain that our Party comrades, despite their experience in the struggle against anti-Soviet elements, despite the numerous warning signals and precautionary signs, proved to be politically short-sighted in the face of the wrecking, espionage-diversionist work of the enemies of the people?

Perhaps our Party comrades have become worse than they were previously, less conscious and less disciplined? No, of course not!

Perhaps they have begun to degenerate? Once again, no! Such an assumption would be totally unfounded.

Then what is the matter? From where does this empty-headedness, carelessness, complacency, and blindness come?

The fact of the matter is that our Party comrades, carried away by economic campaigns and colossal successes on the economic construction front, simply forgot about certain very important facts which Bolsheviks have no right to forget. They forgot about the one basic fact connected with the international position of the USSR and did not notice two very important facts which have a direct relationship regarding the present-day wreckers, spies, diversionists, and killers who shield themselves behind the Party membership card and mask themselves as Bolsheviks.

II. CAPITALIST ENCIRCLEMENT

What are the facts which our Party comrades have forgotten about or which they simply have not noticed?

They have forgotten that Soviet power was victorious in only one-sixth of the world, that five-sixths of the world are in the possession of the capitalist states. They have forgotten that the Soviet Union finds itself encircled by capitalist states. We have an accepted habit of chattering about capitalist encirclement, but people don't want to ponder about what this thing is-capitalist encirclement. Capitalist encirclement-it is not an empty phrase, it is a very real and unpleasant phenomenon. Capitalist encirclement-it means that there is one country, the Soviet Union, which has established at home a Socialist order, and that there are, besides, many countries, bourgeois countries, which continue to carry on the capitalist form of life and which encircle the Soviet Union, waiting for the opportunity to attack it, to crush it, or, in any case-to undermine its might and to weaken it.

It is this main fact that our comrades have forgotten. But it is precisely this fact which determines the basis of the relations between the capitalist encirclement and the Soviet Union.

Take, for example, the bourgeois states. Naive people might think that exceptionally good relations exist between them as states of the same type. But only naive people can think like that. In actual fact, far from neighborly relations exist between them. It has been proved as surely as two times two is four that the bourgeois states send to each other's rear [ask] spies, wreckers, diversionists, and sometimes also killers, who are given the task of penetrating into the institutions and enterprises of these states, of setting up their agencies and "in case of necessity," of disrupting their rear in order to weaken them and to undermine their might. So is the case at the present time. So also was the case in the past. Take, for example, the states in Europe at the time of Napoleon I. France was then swarming with spies and diversionists from the camps of the Russians, Germans, Austrians, and English. And, on the other hand, England, the German states, Austria, and Russia had at that time in their rear no fewer spies and diversionists from the French camp. Agents of England twice made an attempt on the life of Napoleon and several times roused the Vendee peasants in France against the government of Napoleon. And what was the Napoleonic government? A bourgeois government which strangled the French Revolution and retained only those results of the revolution which were advantageous to the big bourgeoisie. Needless to say, the Napoleonic government did not remain in debt to its neighbors and also undertook diversionist measures. So it was in the past, 130 years ago. So the matter stands today, 130 years after Napoleon I. Now France and England are swarming with German spies and diversionists and, on the other hand, Anglo-French spies and diversionists are active in turn in Germany. America is swarming with Japanese spies and diversionists and Japan with American.

Such is the law of the interrelations between bourgeois states.

The question arises, why should the bourgeois states treat the Soviet Socialist state more gently and in a more neighborly manner than towards bourgeois states of the same type? Why should they send to the rear of the Soviet Union fewer spies, wreckers, diversionists, and killers than they send to the rear of the bourgeois states akin to them? From where did this assumption come? Would it not be more true, from the point of view of Marxism, to assume that the bourgeois states would send to the rear of the Soviet Union two and three times more wreckers, spies, diversionists, and killers than to the rear of any bourgeois state?

Is it not clear that for as long as we have capitalist encirclement, we shall have wreckers, spies, diversionists, and killers sent to our rear by agents of foreign states?

All this was forgotten by our Party comrades and, having forgotten about this, they were taken unawares.

That is why the espionage-diversionist work of the Trotskyist agents of the Japano-German secret police was for some of our comrades a complete surprise.

III. CONTEMPORARY TROTSKYISM

Further. In waging the struggle against Trotskyist agents, our Party comrades failed to notice, overlooked, that present-day Trotskyism is not what it was, let us say, seven or eight years ago; that Trotskyism and the Trotskyists have, during this time, undergone a serious evolution which has radically altered the face of Trotskyism; that in view of this in the struggle against Trotskyism the methods of struggle likewise must be radically altered. Our Party comrades have failed to notice that Trotskyism has ceased to be a political tendency within the working class, that from that political tendency within the working class which it was seven or eight years ago, Trotskyism has transformed into a frenzied and unprincipled band of wreckers, diversionists, spies, and killers, acting upon the instructions of the intelligence service organs of foreign states.

What is a political tendency within the working class? A political tendency within the working class is a group or party which has its own definite political physiognomy, a platform, a program; which does not hide and can not hide its views from the working class but, on the contrary, propagates its views openly and honestly before the eyes of the working class; which is not afraid to show its political face before the working class, not afraid to demonstrate its real aims and tasks before the working class but, on the contrary, it frankly goes to the working class in order to convince it of the correctness of its views. Trotskyism in the past, seven or eight years ago, was such a political tendency within the working class-anti-Leninist and therefore profoundly mistaken, it is true-nevertheless, a political tendency.

Can it be said that present-day Trotskyism, the Trotskyism, let us say, of 1936, is a political tendency in the working class? No, it is impossible to say this. Why? Because the present-day Trotskyists are afraid to show their real face before the working class, afraid to reveal to it their real aims and tasks; they assiduously conceal from the working class their political physiognomy, afraid that if the working class finds out their real intentions it will swear at them as people alien from the working class and will drive them away. This, in fact, explains why the basic method of Trotskyist work is not now open and honest propaganda of its views before the working class, but rather the masking of its views: the servile and groveling praise of the views of their opponents, the pharisaical and false trampling of their own views in the mud.

At the trial in 1936, if you remember, Kamenev and Zinoviev flatly denied that they had any kind of political platform. They had a full opportunity to unfold their political platform at the trial. Nevertheless, they did not do so, declaring that they had no political platform whatsoever. There can be no doubt that they both lied in denying that they had a platform. Now even the blind can see that they had a political platform. But why did they deny the existence of any political platform? Because they were afraid to disclose their real political face, they were afraid to demonstrate their real political platform of restoring Capitalism in the USSR; they were afraid that such a platform would arouse revulsion in the working class.

At the trial in 1937, Piatakov, Radek, and Sokolnikov took a different course. They did not deny that the Trotskyists and Zinovievists had a political platform. They admitted they had a definite political platform, admitted it and unfolded in their testimony. But they unfolded it not in order to rally the working class, to rally the people to support the Trotskyist platform, but rather to damn it and brand it as an anti-people and anti-proletarian platform. The restoration of capitalism, the liquidation of the collective farms and state-farms, the re-establishment of a system of exploitation, alliance with the Fascist forces of

Germany and Japan to bring nearer a war with the Soviet Union, a struggle for war and against the policy of peace, the territorial dismemberment of the Soviet Union with the Ukraine to the Germans and the Maritime Province to the Japanese, the scheming for the military defeat of the Soviet Union in the event of an attack on it by hostile states and, as a means for achieving these aims: wrecking, diversionism, industrial terror against the leaders of Soviet power, espionage on behalf of Japano-German Fascist forces-such was the political platform of present-day Trotskyism as unfolded by Piatakov, Radek, and Sokolnikov. Naturally the Trotskyists could not but conceal such a platform from the people, from the working class. And they concealed it not only from the working class, but also from the Trotskyist rank and file as well, and not only from the Trotskyist rank and file, but even from the upper Trotskyist leadership, comprised of a small group of 30 or 40 people. When Radek and Piatakov demanded permission from Trotsky to convene a small conference of 30 or 40 Trotskyists in order to provide information on the character of this platform, Trotsky forbade them to do so, saying that it was inexpedient to speak of the true character of this platform even to a small group of Trotskyists, since such an "operation" might lead to a split.

"Political figures" concealing their views and their platform not only from the working class but also from the Trotskyist rank and file, and not only from the Trotskyist rank and file, but also from the upper leadership of the Trotskyists — such is the physiognomy of contemporary Trotskyism.

But from this it follows that contemporary Trotskyism can no longer be called a political tendency within the working class.

Contemporary Trotskyism is not a political trend within the working class, but an unprincipled and intellectually devoid band of wreckers, diversionists, intelligence agents, spies, and killers; a band of sworn enemies of the working class in the hire of the intelligence service organs of foreign states.

Such is the indisputable result of the evolution of Trotskyism in the past seven or eight years.

Such is the difference between Trotskyism in the past and Trotskyism in the present.

The mistake our Party comrades made lies in the fact they failed to notice this profound difference between Trotskyism in the past and Trotskyism in the present day. They failed to notice that the Trotskyists have long since transformed into highway robbers capable of any villainy, capable of all that is disgusting down to espionage and straight betrayal of their motherland in order to injure the Soviet state and Soviet power. They failed to notice this and were therefore unable to adapt themselves in time to wage a struggle against the Troskyists in a new way, more decisively.

That is why the abominations of the Trotskyists in recent years were for some of our Party comrades such a total surprise.

Further. Finally, our Party comrades failed to notice that there is an important difference between the present-day wreckers and diversionists on the one hand, among whom the Trotskyist agents of Fascism play a rather active role, and the wreckers and diversionists of the time of the Shakhty case, on the other.

Firstly. The Shakhty people and Promparty people were people openly alien to us. They were for the most part former owners of enterprises, former managers under the old employers, former shareholders in joint stock companies, or simply old bourgeois specialists who were openly hostile to us politically. None of our people doubted the authentic political face of these gentlemen. And the Shakhty people themselves did not conceal their dislike for the Soviet system. One can not say the same about the present-day wreckers and diversionists, about the Trotskyists. The present-day wreckers and diversionists, the Trotskyists- these are for the mostly Party people, with Party membership cards in their pockets, people who are formally not alien to us. While the old wreckers came out against our people, the new wreckers, on the contrary, fawn upon our people, praise our people, toady to them in order to worm their way into confidence. The difference is, as you see, vital.

Secondly. The strength of the Shakhty people and the Promparty people lay in the fact that they, more or less, possessed the necessary technical knowledge at a time when our people, lacking such knowledge, were compelled to learn from them. This circumstance gave the wreckers of the Shakhty period a great advantage; it gave them the opportunity to wreck freely and unhindered, gave them the opportunity to deceive our people technically. Not so with the present-day wreckers, with the Trotskyists. The present-day wreckers are not superior in technical knowledge to our people. On the contrary, our people are better trained technically than the present-day wreckers, than the Trotskyists. From the time of the Shakhty period to our day, tens of thousands of real, technically well-versed Bolshevik cadres have grown up among us. One could name thousands and tens of thousands of technically educated Bolshevik leaders, in comparison with whom all these Piatakovs and Livshitses, Shestovs and Boguslavskiis, Muralovs and Drobnises are mere chatterboxes and schoolboys from the standpoint of technical training. Wherein then lies the strength of the contemporary wreckers, the Trotskyists? Their strength lies in the Party card, in their possession of a Party card. Their strength like in the fact that the Party card gains for them political confidence and opens to them all our institutions and organizations. Their advantage lies in the fact that by possessing Party cards and pretending to be friends of Soviet power, they have deceived our people politically, abused confidence, wrecked on the sly, and revealed our state secrets to the enemies of the Soviet Union. The "advantage" is doubtful in its political and moral value, but it is nevertheless an "advantage." This "advantage" explains, substantially, why the Trotskyist wreckers, as people with Party cards and having access to all places in our institutions and organizations, proved such a godsend for the intelligence service organs of foreign states.

The mistake made by some of our Party comrades is that they failed to notice and did not understand this difference between the old and new wreckers, between the Shakhty people and the Trotskyists, and, not noticing this, they were unable to adapt themselves in time to fight with the new wreckers in a new way.

APPENDIX: SPEECH DELIVERED AT MEETING OF VOTERS OF THE STALIN ELECTORAL AREA

Comrades, to tell you the truth, I had no intention of making a speech. But our respected Nikita Sergeyevich [Khrushchov] dragged me, so to speak, to this meeting. "Make a good speech," he said. What shall I talk about, exactly what sort of speech? Everything that had to be said before the elections has already been said and said again in the speeches of our leading comrades, Kalinin, Molotov, Voroshilov, Kaganovich, Yezhov and many other responsible comrades. What can be added to these speeches?

What is needed, they say, are

explanations of certain questions connected with the election campaign. What explanations, on what questions? Everything that had to be explained has been explained and explained again in the well- known appeals of the Bolshevik Party, the Young Communist League, the All-Union Central Trade Union Council, the Osoaviakhim, and the Committee of Physical Culture. What can be added to these explanations?

Of course, one could make a light sort of speech about everything and nothing. *(Amusement.)* Perhaps such a speech would amuse the audience. They say that there are some great hands at such speeches not only over there, in the capitalist countries, but here too, in the Soviet country. *(Laughter and applause.)* But, firstly, I am no great hand at such speeches.

Secondly, is it worth while indulging in amusing things just now when all of us Bolsheviks are, as they say, "up to our necks" in work? I think not.

Clearly, you cannot make a good speech under such circumstances.

However, since I have taken the floor, I will have, of course, to say at least something one way or another. *(Loud applause.)*

First of all, I would like to express my thanks (applause) to the electors for the confidence they have shown in me. *(Applause.)*

I have been nominated as candidate, and the Election Commission of the Stalin Area of the Soviet capital has registered my candidature. This, comrades, is an expression of great confidence. Permit me to convey my profound Bolshevik gratitude for this confidence that you have shown in the Bolshevik Party of which I am a member, and in me personally as a representative of that Party. *(Loud applause.)*

I know what confidence means. It naturally lays upon me new and additional duties and, consequently, new and additional responsibilities. Well, it is not customary among us Bolsheviks to refuse responsibilities. I accept them willingly. *(Loud and prolonged applause.)*

For my part, I would like to assure you, comrades, that you may safely rely on Comrade Stalin. *(Loud and sustained cheers. A voice: "And we all stand for Comrade Stalin!")* You may take it for granted that Comrade Stalin will be able to discharge his duty to the people (applause), to the working class *(applause),* to the peasantry (applause) and to the intelligentsia. *(Applause.)*

Further, comrades, I would like to congratulate you on the occasion of the forthcoming national holiday, the day of the elections to the Supreme Soviet of the Soviet Union. *(Loud applause.)* The forthcoming elections are not merely elections, comrades, they are really a national holiday of our workers, our peasants and our intelligentsia. *(Loud applause.)* Never in the history of the world have there been such really free and really democratic elections—never! History knows no other example like it. *(Applause.)* The point is not that our elections will be universal, equal, secret and direct, although that fact in itself is of great importance. The point is that our universal elections will be carried out as the freest elections and the most democratic of any country in the world.

Universal elections exist and are held in some capitalist countries, too, so-called democratic countries. But in what atmosphere are elections held there? In an atmosphere 0f class conflicts, in an atmosphere of class enmity, in an atmosphere of pressure brought to bear on the electors by the capitalists, landlords, bankers and other capitalist sharks. Such elections, even if they are universal, equal, secret and direct, cannot be called altogether free and altogether democratic elections.

Here, in our country, on the contrary, elections are held in an entirely different atmosphere. Here there are no capitalists and no landlords and, consequently, no pressure is exerted by propertied classes on non-propertied classes. Here elections are held in an atmosphere of collaboration between the workers, the peasants and the intelligentsia, in an atmosphere of mutual confidence between them, in an atmosphere, I would say, of mutual friendship; because there are no capitalists in our country, no landlords, no exploitation and nobody, in fact, to bring pressure to bear on people in order to distort their will.

That is why our elections are the only really free and really democratic elections in the whole world. *(Loud applause.)*

Such free and really democratic elections could arise only on the basis of the triumph of the socialist system, only on the basis of the fact that in our country socialism is not merely being built, but has already become part of life, of the daily life of the people. Some ten years ago the question might still be debated whether socialism could be built in our country or not. Today this is no longer a debatable question. Today it is a matter of facts, a matter of real life, a matter of habits that permeate the whole life of the people. Our mills and factories are being run without capitalists. The work is directed by men and women of the people. That is what we call socialism in practice. In our fields the tillers of the land work without landlords and without kulaks. The work is directed by men and women of the people. That is what we call socialism in daily life, that is what we call a free, socialist life.

It is on this basis that our new, really free and really democratic elections have arisen, elections which have no precedent in the history of mankind.

How then, after this, can one refrain from congratulating you on the occasion of the day of national celebration, the day of the elections to the Supreme Soviet of the Soviet Union! *(Loud, general cheers.)*

Further, comrades, I would like to give you some advice, the advice of a candidate to his electors. If you take capitalist countries you will find that peculiar, I would say, rather strange relations exist there between deputies and voters. As long as the elections are in progress, the deputies flirt with the electors, fawn on them, swear fidelity and make heaps of promises of every kind. It would appear that the deputies are completely dependent on the electors. As soon as the elections are over, and the candidates have become deputies, relations undergo a radical change. Instead of the deputies being dependent on the electors, they become entirely independent. For four or five years, that is, until the next elections, the deputy feels quite free, independent of the people, of his electors. He may pass from one camp to another, he may turn from the right road to the wrong road, he may even become entangled in machinations of a not altogether desirable character, he may turn as many somersaults as he likes—he is independent.

Can such relations be regarded as normal? By no means, comrades. This circumstance was taken into consideration by our Constitution and it made it a law that electors have the right to recall their deputies before the expiration of their term of office if they begin to play monkey tricks, if they turn off the road, or if they forget that they are dependent on the people, on the electors.

This is a wonderful law, comrades. A

deputy should know that he is the servant of the people, their emissary in the Supreme Soviet, and he must follow the line laid down in the mandate given him by the people. If he turns off the road, the electors. are entitled to demand new elections, and as to the deputy who turned off the road, they have the right to blackball him. *(Laughter and applause.)* This is a wonderful law. My advice, the advice of a candidate to his electors, is that they remember this electors' right, the right to recall deputies before the expiration of their term of office, that they keep an eye on their deputies, control them and, if they should take it into their heads to turn off the right road, get rid of them and demand new elections. The government is obliged to appoint new elections. My advice is to remember this law and to take advantage of it should need arise.

And, lastly, one more piece of advice from a candidate to his electors. What in general must one demand of one's deputies, selecting from all possible demands the most elementary?

The electors, the people, must demand that their deputies should remain equal to their tasks, that in their work they should not sink to the level of political philistines, that in their posts they should remain political figures of the Lenin type, that as public figures they should be as clear and definite as Lenin was *(applause),* that they should be as fearless in battle and as merciless towards the enemies of the people as Lenin was *(applause),* that they should be free from all panic, from any semblance of panic, when things begin to get complicated and some danger or other looms on the horizon, that they should be as free from all semblance of panic as

Lenin was *(applause)*, that they should be as wise and deliberate in deciding complex problems requiring a comprehensive orientation and a comprehensive weighing of all pros and cons as Lenin was *(applause)*, that they should be as upright and honest as Lenin was *(applause)*, that they should love their people as Lenin did. *(Applause.)*

Can we say that all the candidates are public figures precisely of this kind? I would not say so. There are all sorts of people in the world, there are all sorts of public figures in the world. There are people of whom you cannot say what they are, whether they are good or bad, courageous or timid, for the people heart and soul or for the enemies of the people. There are such people and there are such public figures. They are also to be found among us, the

Bolsheviks. You know yourselves, comrades— there are black sheep in every family. *(Laughter and applause.)* Of people of this indefinite type, people who resemble political philistines rather than political figures, people of this vague, amorphous type, the great Russian writer, Gogol, rather aptly said: "Vague sort of people, says he, neither one thing nor the other, you can't make head or tail of them, they are neither Bogdan in town nor Seliphan in the country." *(Laughter and applause.)* There are also some rather apt popular sayings about such indefinite people and public figures: "A middling sort of man—neither fish nor flesh" *(general laughter and applause),* "neither a candle for god nor a poker for the devil." *(General laughter and applause.)*

I cannot say with absolute certainty that

among the candidates (I beg their pardon, of course) and among our public figures there are not people who more than anything resemble political philistines, who in character and make-up resemble people of the type referred to in the popular saying: "Neither a candle for god nor a poker for the devil." *(Laughter and applause.)*

I would like you, comrades, to exercise systematic influence on your deputies, to impress upon them that they must constantly keep before them the great image of the great Lenin and imitate Lenin in all things. *(Applause.)*

The functions of the electors do not end with the elections. They continue during the whole term of the given Supreme Soviet. I have already mentioned the law which empowers the electors to recall their deputies before the expiration of their term of office if they should turn off the right road. Hence it is the duty and right of the electors to keep their deputies constantly under their control and to impress upon them that they must under no circumstances sink to the level of political philistines, impress upon their deputies that they must be like the great Lenin. *(Applause.)*

Such, comrades, is my second piece of advice to you, the advice of a candidate to his electors. *(Loud and sustained applause and cheers. All rise and turn towards the government box, to which Comrade Stalin proceeds from the platform. Voices: "Hurrah for the great Stalin!" "Hurrah for Comrade Stalin!" "Long live Comrade Stalin!" "Long live the first of the Leninists, candidate for the Soviet of the Union, Comrade Stalin!")*

www.ingramcontent.com/pod-product-compliance
Lightning Source LLC
Chambersburg PA
CBHW020330290526
45785CB00007B/3000